CRANES
at Work

D. R. Addison

PowerKiDS
press

New York

To my little truck experts, Deming, Riley, and Hannah

Published in 2009 by The Rosen Publishing Group, Inc.
29 East 21st Street, New York, NY 10010

First Edition

Editor: Joanne Randolph
Book Design: Greg Tucker
Photo Researcher: Jessica Gerweck

Photo Credits: Cover, pp. 5, 7, 9, 13, 15, 17, 19, 21, 23, 24 Shutterstock.com; p. 11 www.iStockphoto.com.

Library of Congress Cataloging-in-Publication Data

Addison, D. R.
  Cranes at work / D. R. Addison. — 1st ed.
      p. cm. — (Big trucks)
  Includes index.
  ISBN 978-1-4358-2703-5 (library binding) — ISBN 978-1-4358-3089-9 (pbk.)
 ISBN 978-1-4358-3095-0 (6-pack)
  1. Cranes, derricks, etc.—Juvenile literature. I. Title.
  TJ1363.A75 2009
  621.8'73—dc22
                                                    2008023560

Manufactured in the United States of America

Contents

Here is a crane ready for work. Have you ever seen a crane?

Cranes have a big job. They lift and carry heavy loads.

Cranes work hard at the **construction site** all day.

Some cranes are small. This crane lifts and carries logs.

11

Some cranes are big. This crane is helping build **windmills**.

13

Cranes have a big arm,
which can be made longer.
The arm moves up and
down, too.

15

Many cranes have a rope, or cable, with a big **hook** at the end.

This crane has a place for people to stand. It lifts workers up to high places.

This crane is lifting supplies. It places them on the **roof** of the building.

Time to go home for the day. This crane will be back at work tomorrow!

Words to Know

construction site

hook

roof

windmill

Index

Web Sites

Due to the changing nature of Internet links, PowerKids Press has developed an online list of Web sites related to the subject of this book. This site is updated regularly. Please use this link to access the list:

www.powerkidslinks.com/bigt/crane/